I Was Just About To Go To Bed

written by
Lucy McClymont

illustrated by
Wallace Keller

HARCOURT BRACE & COMPANY

Orlando Atlanta Austin Boston San Francisco Chicago Dallas New York
Toronto London

So I have my teddy and my bunny.
But I don't have my duck.

So I have my teddy and my bunny and my duck.
But I don't have my light.

So I have my teddy and my bunny and my duck and my light.
But I don't have my cup.

So I have my teddy and my bunny and my duck and my light and my cup.

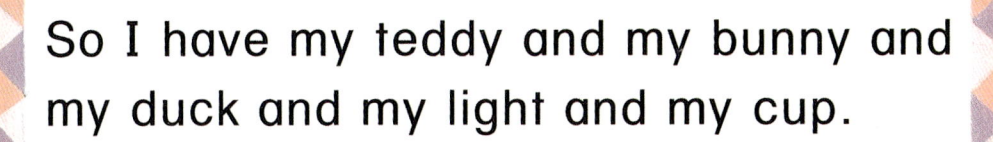

I was just about to go to bed.
But I don't have a bed!